texts from  s

The Friends and Family Edition

texts from mittens

The Friends and Family Edition

Angie Bailey

Andrews McMeel
PUBLISHING®

Mittens: A text-happy indoor tuxie who loves *Judge Judy*, liver treats, fancy drinking fountains . . . and creating unnecessary drama.

Mom: A single working woman who likes to dabble in online dating and (usually) sees through Mittens' schemes.

Earl: The simple-minded Lab-mix "filthy hound" who lives with Mittens and his mom. Earl likes to chase squirrels.

Stumpy: Mittens's wild best friend who lives down the block. He's a large indoor-outdoor, female-loving orange tabby who's usually high on catnip and looking for a quick buck.

Grandma: The bearer of treats and presents. Mittens makes special allowances for Grandma when it comes to taking photos, wearing costumes, and other degrading activities.

Drunk Patty: The always happy, sometimes tipsy next-door neighbor who adores Mittens and feeds him and Earl when Mom is gone. Mittens is annoyed by everything that is Drunk Patty.

Fiona: Mittens's sweet and patient girlfriend, a silver tabby who lives in the neighborhood. She brings out the vulnerable side of The Mittens.

For Cosmo

Grandma, are you still coming for a visit?

Yes, Mittens! I'm looking forward to it!

Will you watch me stand between the curtain and the window and tell me how mysterious I look?

If you'd like me to.

I definitely would.

See you soon.

Roger that, Grandma. #overandout

1

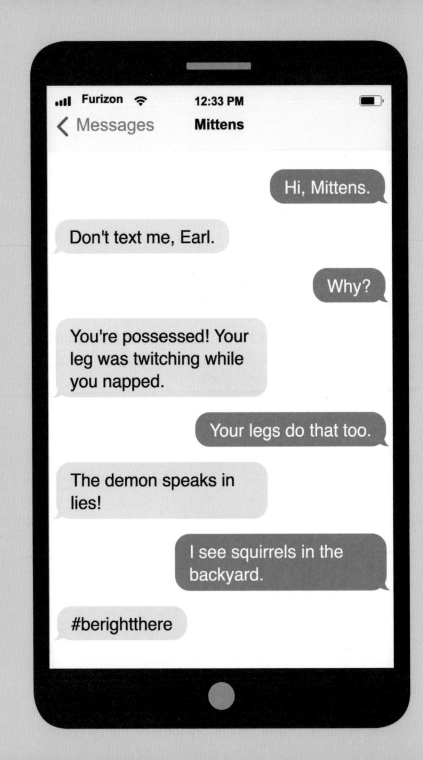

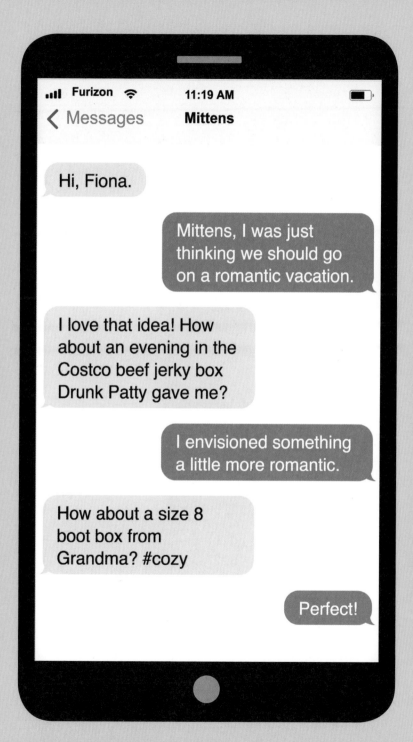

Mom, my day is bad.

What's wrong, Mitty?

I was watching birds and my claw got stuck in the window screen.

And then a gang of blue jays mocked me from the feeder. One of them told me I'd soon be swimming with the fishes.

That's not what he said.

So now you can suddenly speak blue jay? #asif

What is that dreadful noise coming from your yard, Drunk Patty?

Mitttyyy! I'm playing my kazoooo!

Well, kazoo inside. I'm trying to nap!

But I'm waiting for the pizzzza delivery!

Pizza? Will there be extra cheese? I may be open to negotiations regarding the kazoo.

I'd also like to request full custody of the box.

Earl, have I told you you're a good dog?

No. You call me a filthy hound.

You misunderstand me. So -- I fancy a bag of croissants on the kitchen counter.

You're not allowed on the counter, Mittens.

Right, but no one ever said good dogs aren't. I'll pay you in croissant.

My generosity astounds even me.

I'm embarrassed that Stumpy can jump higher than me, Fiona.

Mittens, you're a very good jumper. Don't compare yourself to other cats.

BUT I CAN'T HELP IT. I DON'T WANT YOU TO THINK STUMPY IS TOUGHER THAN ME.

I don't! Now calm down. You type in all caps when you're really anxious.

no i don't.

Yes, this is Mittens. I'd like to order three rolls of paper towels. #notthecheapstuff

We're going to unroll them at my party.

Mitty, this is Grandma.

Curses! I thought I was texting the grocery delivery service!

I can bring you paper towels, Mittens.

Thanks Grandma. Bring liver treats too. #notthecheapstuff

11

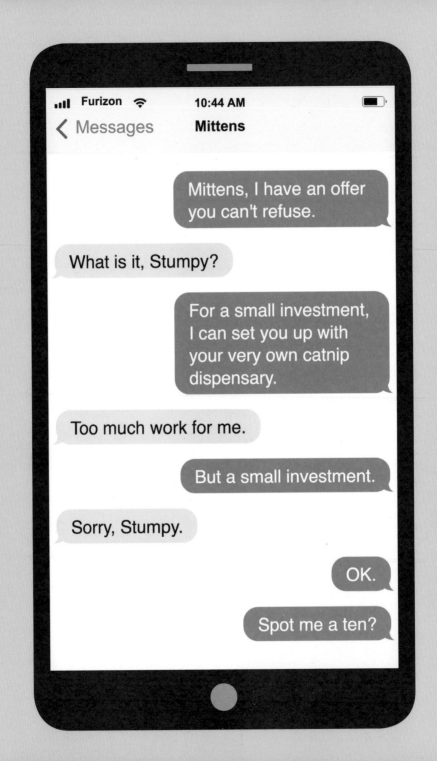

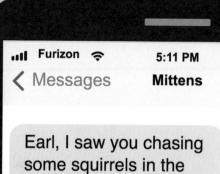

Earl, I saw you chasing some squirrels in the backyard this afternoon.

I like to chase squirrels.

One keeps giving me the evil eye. He's got a scruffy tail and looks like his name might be Vito. Can you put in a good word for me? Just to be safe? #vouchforthemittens

Sure, Mittens.

Thanks, filthy hound. I mean Earl. #respect

13

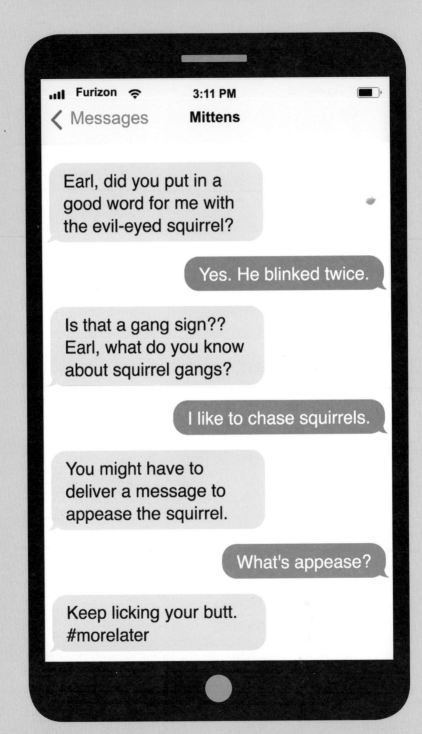

14

Earl, I want you to let the head squirrel know I will leave corn chips on the patio for him, as a sign of respect.

Can I have corn chips?

Earl, just do what I ask and I'll make sure you get some corn chips.

What do you want me to do again?

Never mind. My fate is sealed. #deathbysquirrel

Can I have corn chips?

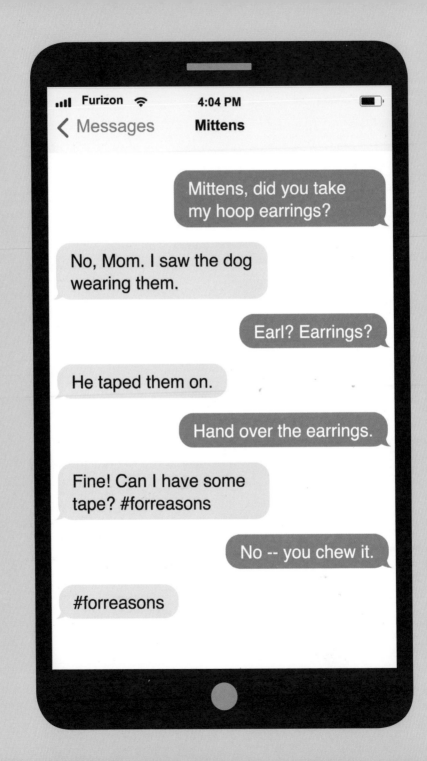

Grandma, Drunk Patty said you won big at the casino last night.

I did! I stayed at the craps table all night!

Grandma!

Did they at least have litter on the table so you could cover up your business?

Craps is a casino game! My dad used to play street craps.

#stoptalkinggrandma

Mom, I'm thinking of getting hair extensions.

What prompted this?

I saw them on an infomercial. I feel like I'd increase my fancy factor by at least 59%.

I don't think they make them for cats, Mitty.

What does the hair extension industry have against cats?

#haircomesinjustice
#thiefoffancy

Grandma, would you buy me a lottery ticket?

Why would you want a lottery ticket, Mittens?

They're "scratch off" tickets, right?

Some are. You can win money, you know.

I don't care about the money. I just want to scratch them.

Or maybe you could set up a trust fund for me. I'll trust you'll use it to buy treats for me.

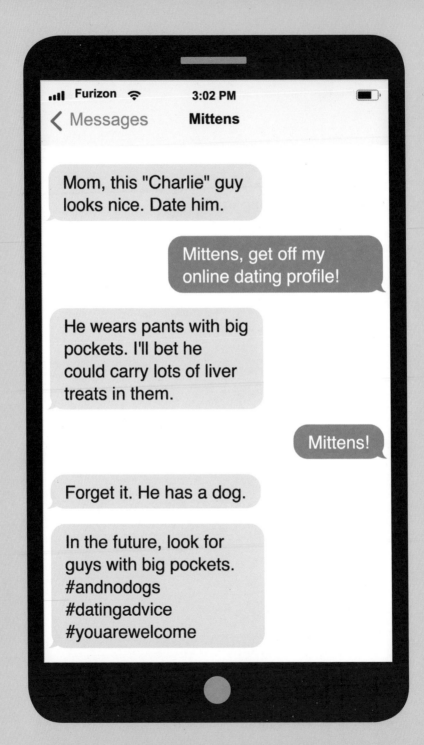

Stumpy, where are you? You were supposed to be here an hour ago.

I have an excellent excuse, my friend.

I'll bet you do. I'll bet it has something to do with a lady cat.

Not this time. I fell asleep with my face inside a smelly, old slipper.

Why didn't you tell me that in the first place? #totallylegit

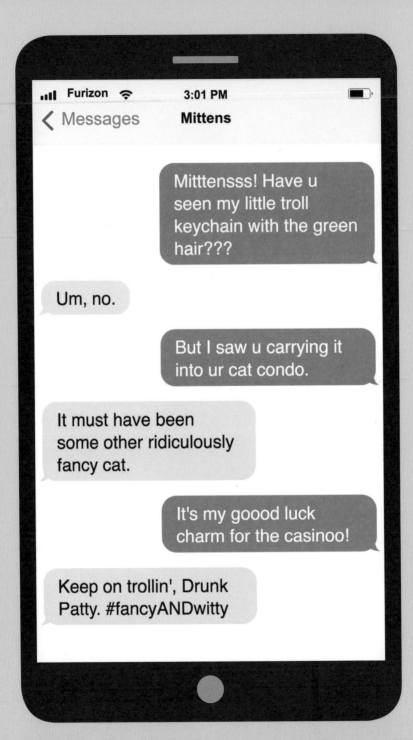

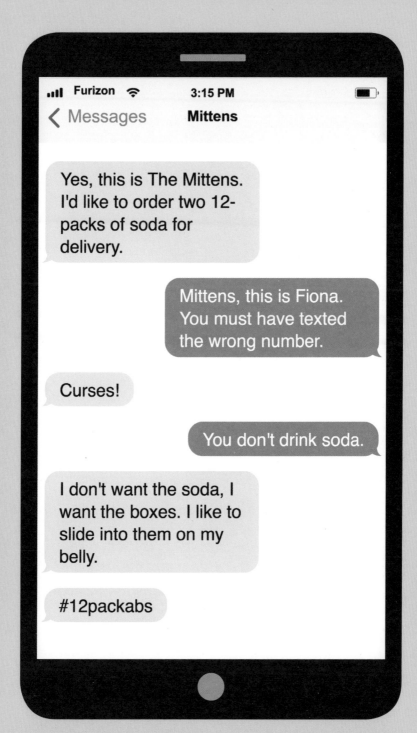

Yes, this is The Mittens. I'd like to order two 12-packs of soda for delivery.

Mittens, this is Fiona. You must have texted the wrong number.

Curses!

You don't drink soda.

I don't want the soda, I want the boxes. I like to slide into them on my belly.

#12packabs

33

Stumpy, come over and watch Judge Judy with me.

No can do, Mitts. I have some rush orders. My cat condo is piled high with 'nip I need to sort and bag for customers.

You're always working, Stumpy. That is, when you're not spending time with the lady cats.

That's right! I'm either working or WORKING IT! LOL.

#ihaveallmyshots

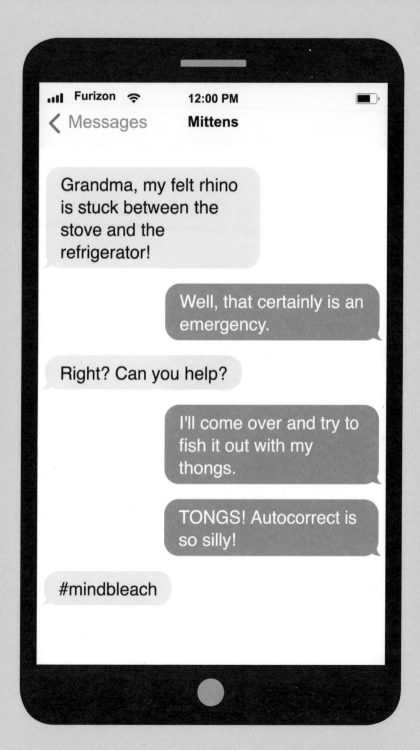

Earl, I think we should form an alliance.

What's an alliance?

It means we come together for the greater good of both of us.

It means you stand by the fridge and I jump from your back and grab our treat bags from the upper cabinet.

I like alliances. Can I have two of them?

Just meet me in the kitchen. #dogproblems

38

Hey, Drunk Patty -- do you have any shampoo bottle lids? I'm playing soccer and lost my last lid under the fridge.

Yess! I havve a greeen one and a bluue one!

I'll take both. Put them through the mail slot.

I'lll bee over when I finnish drinking my bar.

Beer! Autocorrect!

I think you were right the first time. #booya

Mom! Raccoons are at the window! They want to rob us! They're wearing masks!

Mitty, all raccoons wear masks.

So ALL raccoons are robbers? This is a national emergency!

Calm down. It's OK.

For YOU. YOU have nothing to steal! I'm the one with the valuable collection of rare shampoo bottle lids!

Mom, the raccoons are back and they want my felt rhino!

They'll go away.

They're in our garbage!

Fine. I'll go out and replace the can's lid.

You'll face the bandits when they're stealing garbage, but not when my felt rhino is at risk??

You probably want to join their raccoon gang! Who are you???

Are you going to meet up with your sketchy raccoon gang friends tonight, Mom?

Mitty, I'm not going to be in a raccoon gang.

Maybe Grandma will make you a sketchy bandit mask.

Mittens, I'm serious. Go to bed. I'm not a bandit. Love you, Mitty.

Love you too, Mama.

#stillsketchy #hidingvaluables

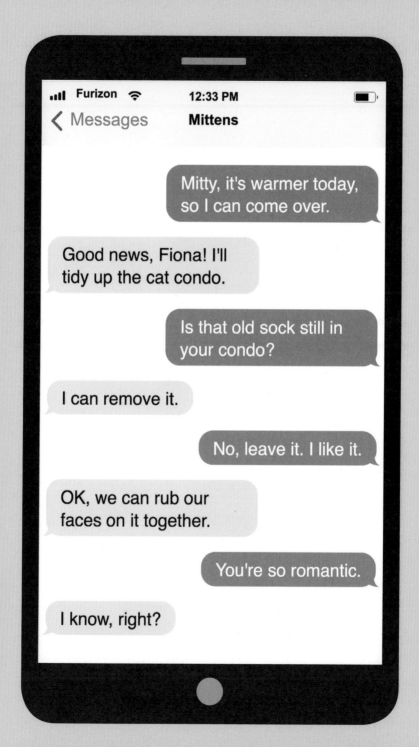

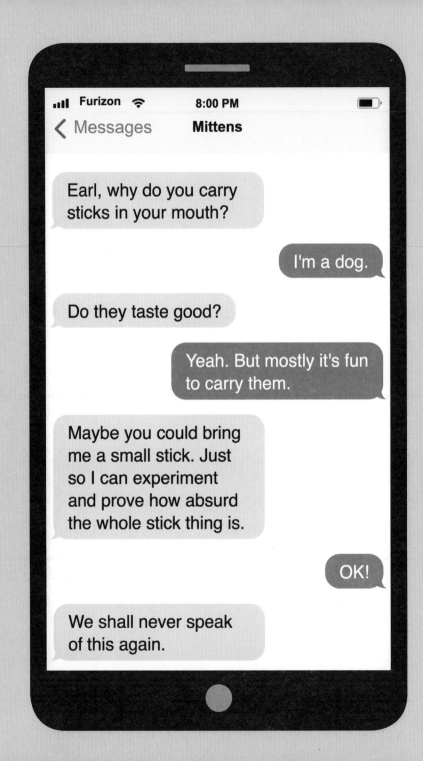

Stumpy doesn't have a grandma.

Poor Stumpy.

I know! Who gives him extra ear rubs and slips him buttered roll bites?

Maybe I can be Stumpy's grandma! Don't you think that's a nice idea, Mittens?

Now is not the time to start making irrational decisions, Grandma. #alltherolls

Fiona, I'm writing a love poem for you.

That's so sweet, Mitty!

I know, right?

But here's the thing: I can't find a word that rhymes with "Fiona."

That is a challenge.

Arizona? Barcelona? No -- those aren't good.

Maybe you could change your name to Pat?

Earl, I can hear you licking your rear from the next room.

That's good.

No it's not! I don't want to hear your filthy butt-bathing.

Mittens, this morning you bathed your butt in front of me.

That's different. For me, it's called "fancy posterior maintenance." #lookitup

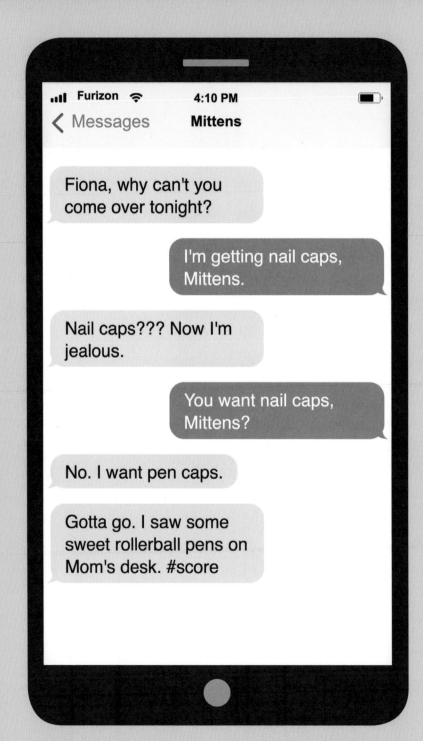

Mitts, I have an idea for a new side business.

Another one, Stumpy? Aren't running 'nip, being my talent manager, and other side hustles enough?

Listen. People always leave clothes behind at my family's laundromat. I can capitalize and sell the pieces to my feline friends for naps! Sliding scale available, of course.

Totally on board. #dibsontowel

Grandma, can you make the dog return Mr. Fuzzy?

Earl has your blanket?

He stole it and now he's drooling his filthy mouth juice all over it!

Aw, he's your brother.

No way -- he's my smelly, disgusting nut!

You don't have those anymore, Mitty. LOL.

MUTT! Autocorrect! #aghast

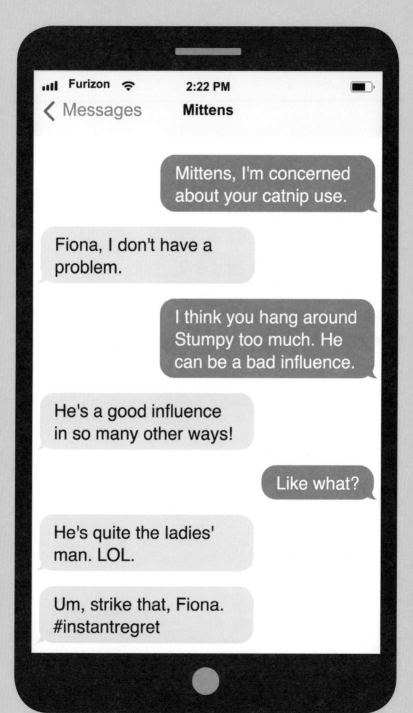

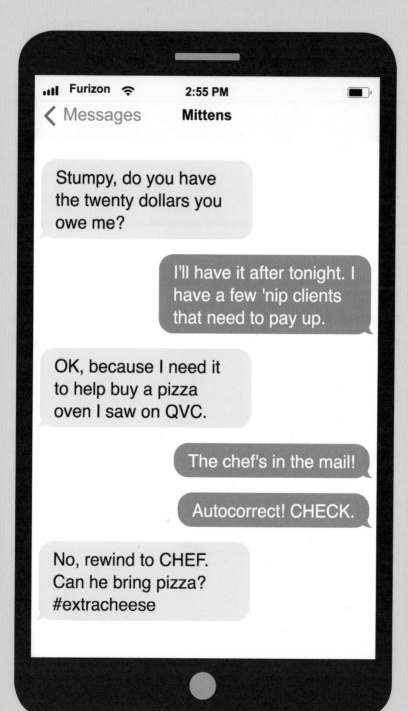

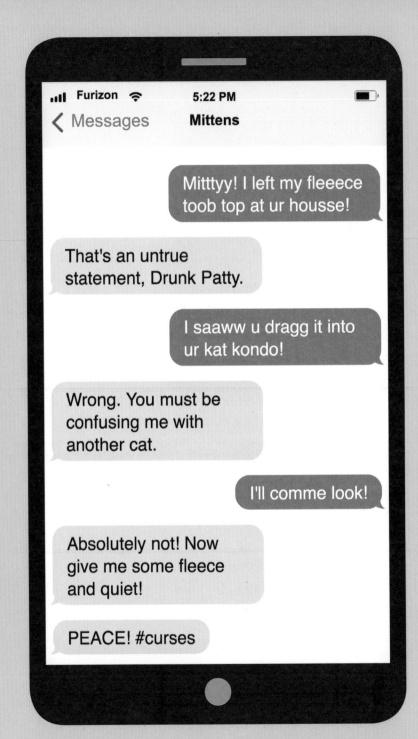

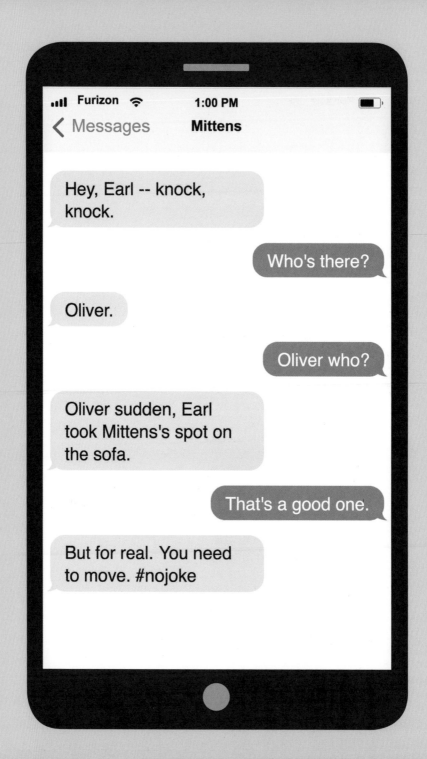

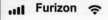

Code red, Grandma! I just found out I'm color blind!

It's OK, Mittens. All cats can only see limited colors.

How will I get through the rest of my lives?? Will I have to walk around with a tiny stick to find my way??

Mittens, you're just fine.

You might have to come over to reassure me. #bringdonuts #ihopeicanseethem

69

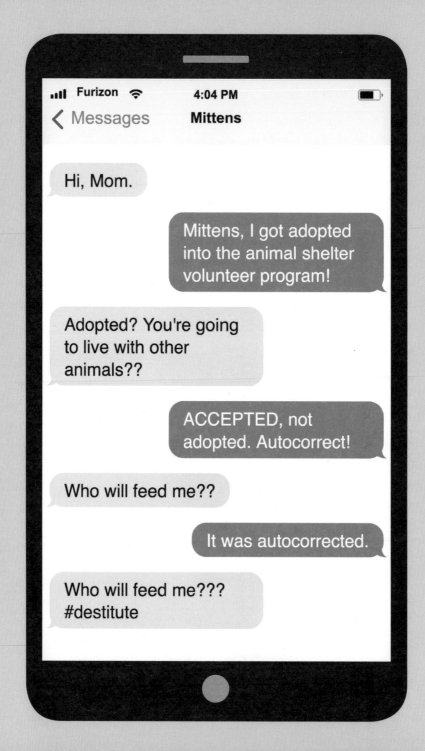

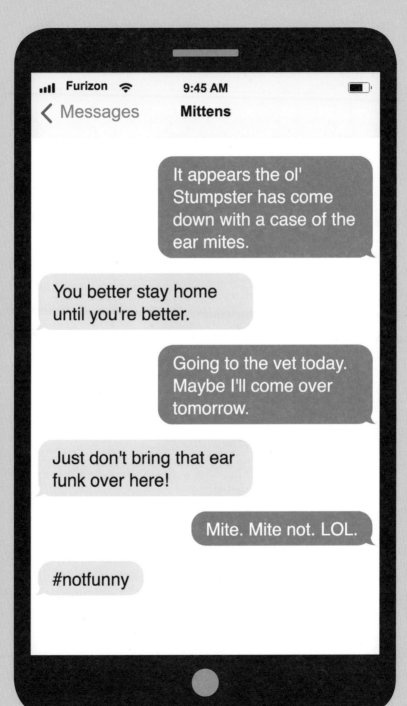

Earl, let's discuss our letter to management.

> Why are we writing and who is management?

I know you're a dog and all, but I need you to stay with me here. We want management (Mom) to provide more treats.

> That sounds good.

> Who's management?

I'll just sign your name. #dogproblems

73

Hey, Drunk Patty -- do you have any extra 12-pack boxes lying around? I need some fresh napping boxes.

Of course I do, Mittyyy!

Great. Leave them by the back door and go back home.

When I waz a little gorilla, I used 2 lovve 2 sleeep in boxes too!

GIRL! Autocorrrect! LOL!

Or is it??

Fiona, I like your new collar. It's so fancy!

Thank you, Mittens!

I hope the fancy new collar doesn't mean you're looking for a new boyfriend. I would be devastated!

No way, Mitty! You're the only guy for me!

Good!

BTW, can I borrow that collar sometime? #sofancy

So are you coming over tonight, Stumpy?

No, I have to spend the night in my family's laundromat because they saw a mouse.

#notfair

It's my job in the family business. Gotta do my part.

They didn't say anything about NOT having lady cats over, though. LOL. #warmtowels #fluffcycle

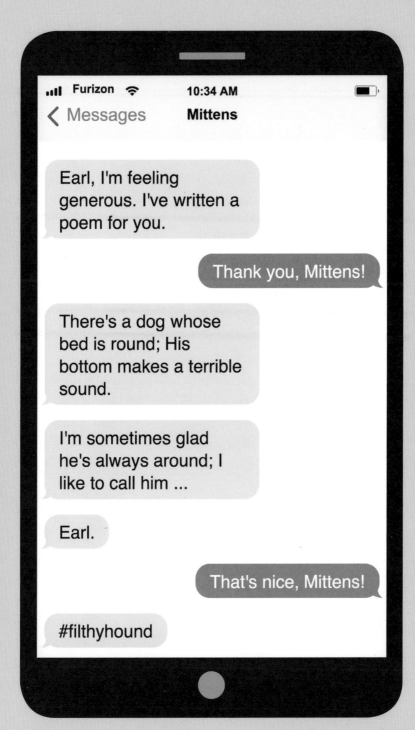

Mother, the filthy hound is so gassy. I fear I will suffocate from the stench.

> Mittens, go into a room where Earl is not.

I want to be in this room! Why do I have to suffer?

We'd be rich if we could bottle and smell all his gas!

Autocorrect! SELL!

Fine. I'll go into another room.

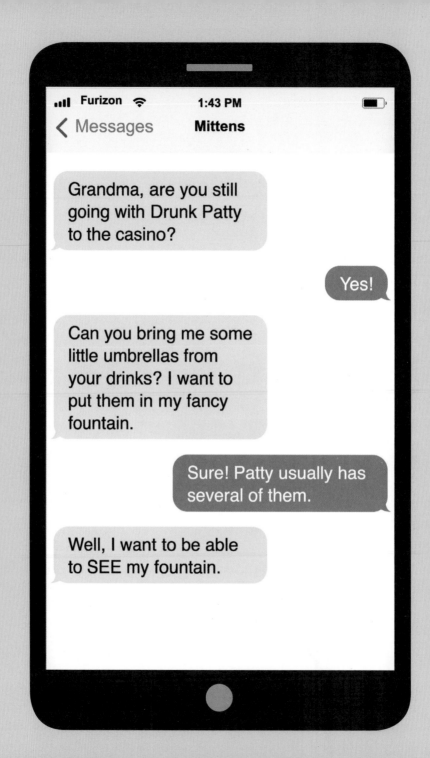

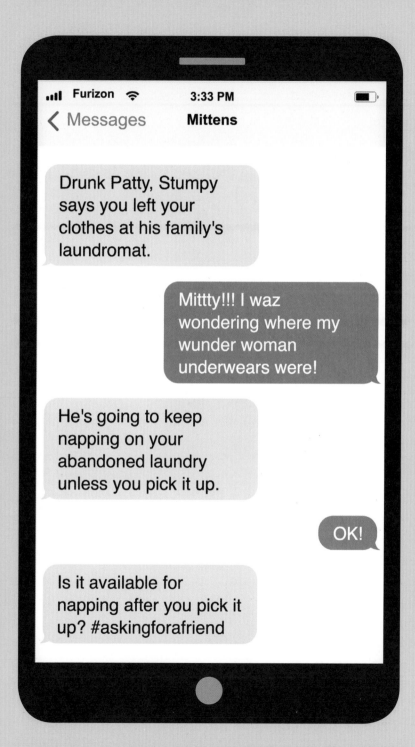

83

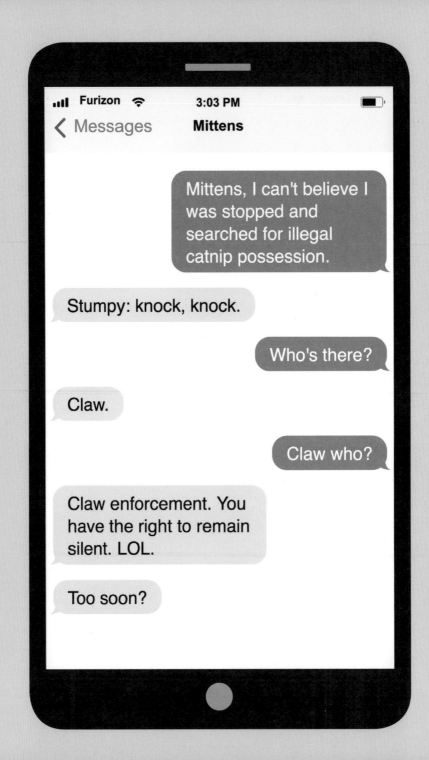

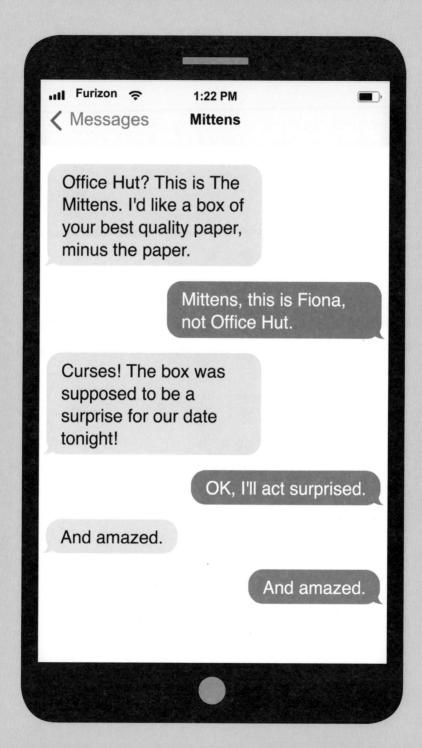

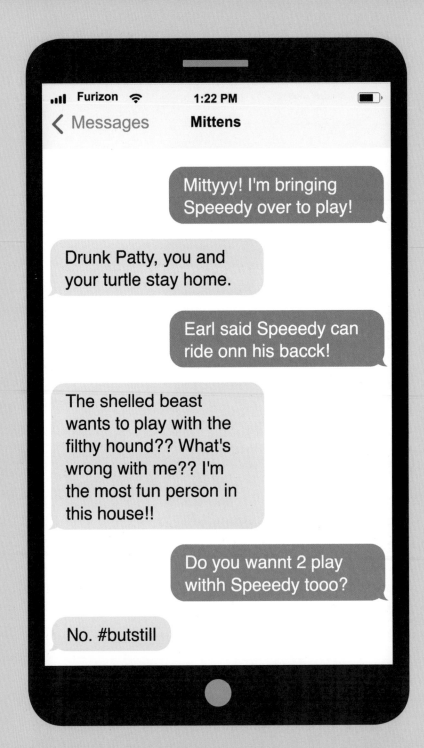

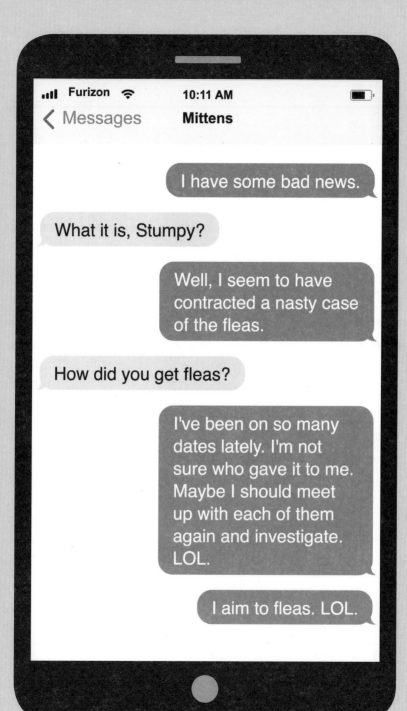

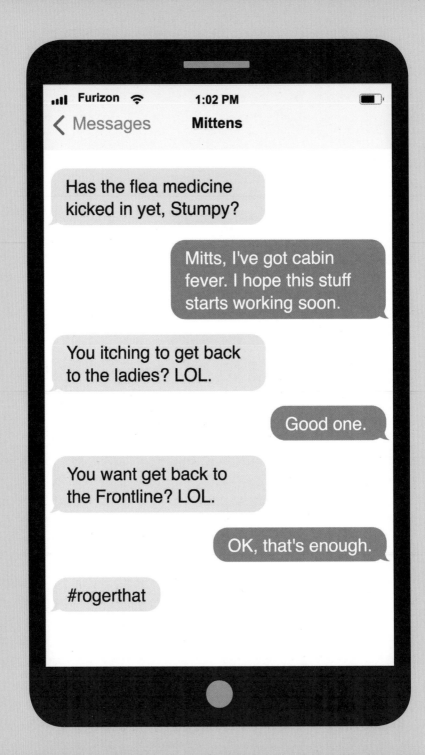

Mom, there's a little piece of poo stuck to my "exit door." Come home and help me! #urgent

Mittens, this is Fiona.

Curses! My girlfriend doesn't need to know such delicate details!

It's OK, Mittens. Yesterday I stepped in some fresh poo before I covered it up.

Really?? YOU stepped in poo? That's amazing. I love you, Fiona.

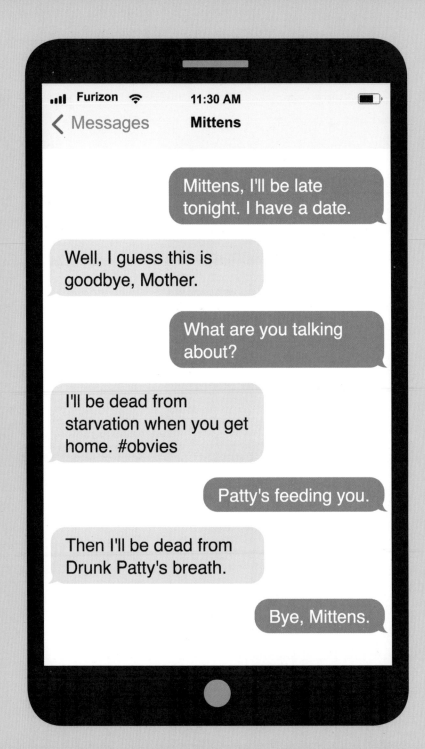

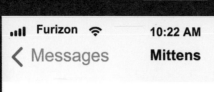

Mitts, as your talent manager, I've recently updated your contract.

Updates, Stumpy?

I added a clause that allows me to have a cut of any promotional catnip you receive.

Bring it over. I'll want to put on my little monocle and check out the small print. We should NIP any issues in the BUD.

Mittens, my friend, you're goin' places.

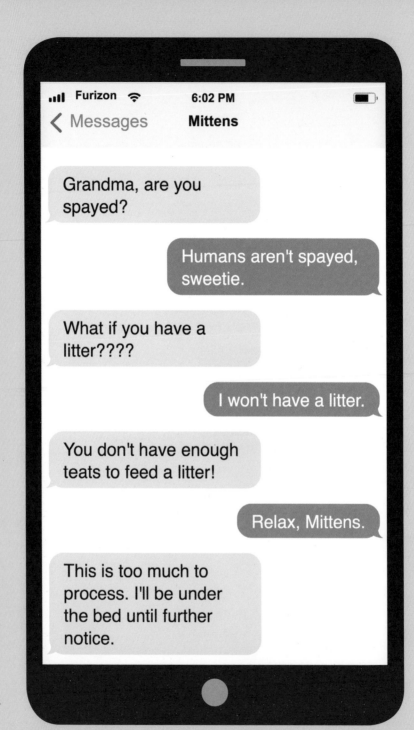

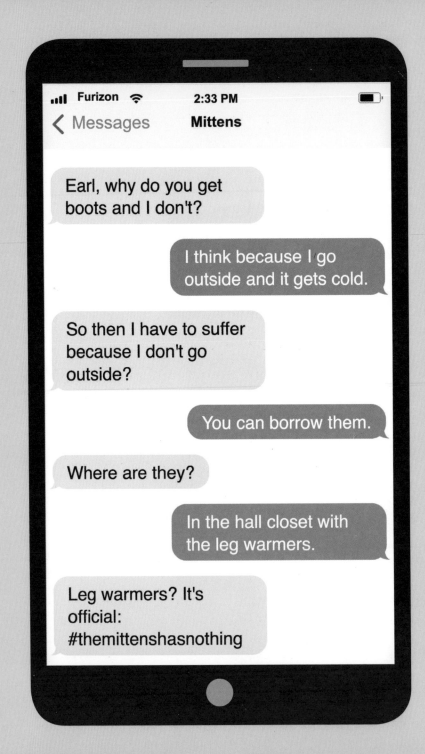

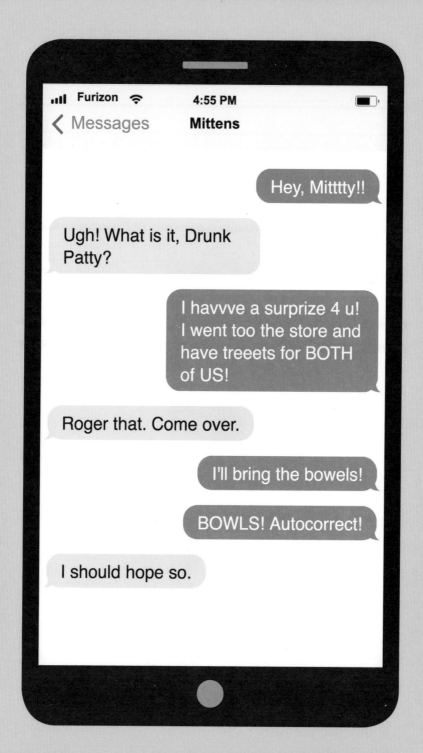

Fiona, would you bring me some milk jug rings? I'm fresh out.

My family drinks almond milk. It doesn't have those rings.

You've never had your very own milk jug rings?? I can't believe my girlfriend is living with such hardship!

Mittens, it's OK -- really.

This is an outrage! I'm texting ASPCA right now to report this atrocity! #stillcomeover

I found the cutest hat for you at the doll shop!

Grandma, I think you have the wrong number.

Mittens! It's so cute! It's red and blue knit!

You know I love you, but it sounds horrific.

It has little ear flaps!

Fine. I'll wear it. At least the ear flaps will shield me from the certain mockery of my friends. #laughingstock

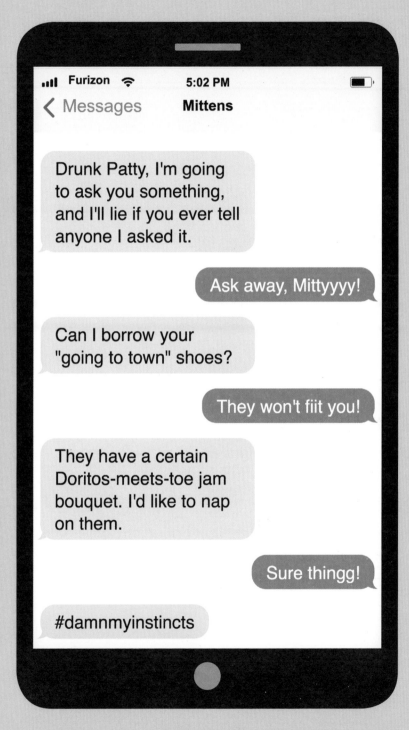

Stumpy, do you want to come over tonight and have a double date with Fiona and me?

Sure. Bernice is my date tonight. She has a beauty of a sister from the same litter. Should I bring her?

Um, I have a girlfriend.

I meant for ME! LOL! Just kidding!

Better put aside some extra treats, though. #justincase

Stumpy, do you want to come over tonight? Mom's making a blanket fort.

That sounds like a good time, Mitts. I'll bring the 'nip.

Mom says we have to promise to not swat at her when she walks by the fort.

Like we can undo thousands of years of cat behavior. Humans are so simple. LOL.

#rogerthat

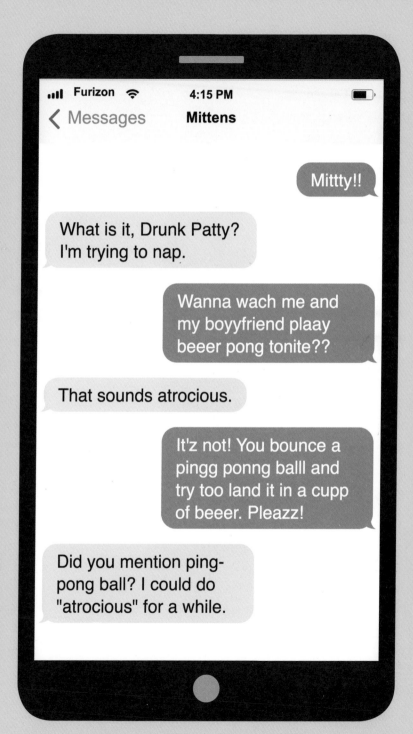

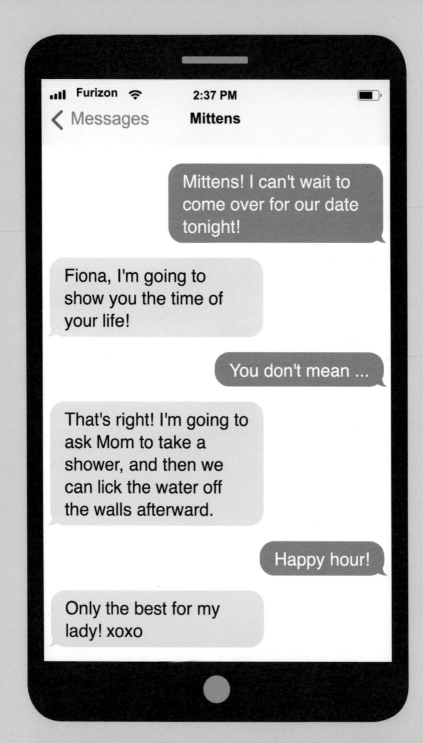

Mom, it's thundering and I can't find Mr. Fuzzy. #blanketcrisis

Mittens, your blanket is folded on my bed.

Not that I'm scared or anything. #tough

Not that I wish you'd come home early or anything.

I know, Mitty. I'll be home soon. Love you.

Love you too, Mama.

Many thanks to my exceptionally supportive friends and family (human and feline). Without their encouragement and inspiration, this book wouldn't have been possible. Much gratitude to my literary agent, Sorche Fairbank, who makes the magic happen.

Andrews McMeel Publishing
a division of Andrews McMeel Universal
1130 Walnut Street, Kansas City, Missouri 64106

www.andrewsmcmeel.com

19 20 21 22 23 TEN 10 9 8 7 6 5 4 3 2 1

ISBN: 978-1-5248-5172-9

Library of Congress Control Number: 2019934182

Editor: Melissa Zahorsky
Art Director/Designer: Sierra Stanton
Production Editor: Jasmine Lim
Production Manager: Tamara Haus

ATTENTION: SCHOOLS AND BUSINESSES

Andrews McMeel books are available at quantity discounts with bulk purchase for educational, business, or sales promotional use. For information, please e-mail the Andrews McMeel Publishing Special Sales Department: specialsales@amuniversal.com.